Digital Couponing Masterclass

Digital Couponing Masterclass

Matthew Petchinsky

1

Digital Couponing Masterclass: Your Step-by-Step Guide to Black Friday Savings

By: Matthew Petchinsky

Introduction

The Evolution from Paper Coupons to Digital Mastery

Not long ago, saving money meant scissors, Sunday newspapers, and bulky coupon binders. Shoppers clipped, sorted, and carried stacks of paper slips into crowded grocery stores, hoping to shave a few dollars off their weekly bill. This process was time-consuming, often frustrating, and limited to whatever a store printed or allowed in its weekly flyer.

Today, that world has transformed. The rise of smartphones, apps, and online shopping platforms has revolutionized couponing into something far more powerful: **digital couponing**. Instead of paper stacks, savings now live inside sleek apps, browser extensions, retailer reward systems, and email alerts. Instead of hoping a cashier will honor a crumpled slip, shoppers now click, tap, and scan barcodes with precision. This digital shift doesn't just make couponing easier—it makes it smarter, faster, and infinitely more rewarding.

Digital couponing is no longer a niche hobby. It is a **modern skillset**, one that savvy consumers use to unlock hundreds, even thousands of dollars in annual savings. When mastered, digital couponing becomes a form of financial strategy, allowing you to stretch every dollar and access exclusive deals hidden from the casual shopper.

Why Black Friday and Cyber Monday Are Prime Coupon Events

Nowhere is the power of digital couponing more visible than during **Black Friday** and **Cyber Monday**, the twin juggernauts of modern retail. These events mark the most competitive shopping period of the year, where retailers slash prices to attract holiday shoppers—and where digital coupons amplify those discounts to levels unimaginable in the paper-coupon era.

Black Friday, once synonymous with chaotic in-store doorbusters, has largely migrated online. Retailers flood their websites with timed flash deals, coupon codes, and stackable offers. Cyber Monday builds on this energy, focusing entirely on e-commerce exclusives and online coupon opportunities. Together, they form the perfect storm of **digital couponing potential**: high demand, aggressive discounts, and a flood of promotional codes designed to capture your attention.

But here's the key: most shoppers barely scratch the surface of these savings. They grab one coupon code and think they've scored big, not realizing that seasoned couponers stack codes, layer app rewards, and time their purchases across multiple platforms. That's where *Digital Couponing Masterclass* comes in.

What You'll Gain

This book isn't about clipping a coupon here or there—it's about **mastering a system**. You'll learn how to:

- Discover hidden coupon sources beyond the obvious websites.
- Use tools and extensions that automate deal-finding.
- Stack discounts across multiple platforms for exponential savings.
- Time purchases to align with unadvertised price drops.
- Organize your digital coupons into a streamlined, efficient system.

By the end, you won't just be saving money—you'll be commanding it. Black Friday and Cyber Monday will no longer feel overwhelming or opportunistic; they'll feel like **your battlefield, your game board, and your victory**.

This is the new age of couponing. Welcome to your masterclass.

Chapter 1: Where to Find High-Value Digital Coupons

Digital couponing begins with one essential skill: **knowing where to look**. High-value coupons don't simply fall into your lap; they are strategically placed across platforms, apps, and communities where only the attentive shopper finds them. This chapter reveals the core hunting grounds for digital coupons and teaches you how to separate the **ordinary discounts** from the **golden deals** that deliver massive savings during Black Friday and beyond.

1.1 Retailer Websites & Loyalty Programs

Most major retailers—Amazon, Walmart, Target, Best Buy, Macy's, Kohl's, and others—publish exclusive digital coupons directly on their websites. These appear as **promo banners**, pop-up offers, or codes tied to specific product categories.

But the real treasures hide inside **loyalty programs**:

- **Target Circle**, **Kohl's Rewards**, **CVS ExtraCare**, and **Walgreens Balance Rewards** all issue rotating digital coupons accessible only through your account dashboard or app.
- Loyalty programs often include **exclusive pre-Black Friday access** to deals or "member-only" coupons that are stackable with public offers.
- Many retailers deliver **personalized coupons** based on your shopping history, offering deeper savings on items you're most likely to buy.

Pro Tip: Always sign up with a secondary email account dedicated to couponing. This keeps your main inbox uncluttered while ensuring you never miss exclusive loyalty deals.

1.2 Coupon Aggregator Websites

Aggregator platforms serve as **coupon hubs**, compiling codes and offers from across the web. While some sites recycle expired codes, the top-tier ones verify validity before posting:

- **RetailMeNot** – Known for breadth, offering everything from major department stores to niche brands.
- **Coupons.com** – A hybrid of printable and digital coupons, now deeply integrated into grocery and retail apps.
- **Honey's Droplist** – Tracks prices and automatically applies coupons at checkout (particularly useful for Amazon).
- **Slickdeals** – A forum-style site where users share verified codes and stacking tricks, often within minutes of release.

Pro Tip: Bookmark at least two aggregator sites, and cross-check coupon codes across both. This minimizes the chance of relying on expired or duplicate offers.

1.3 Browser Extensions & Automation Tools

If hunting down codes manually feels overwhelming, let **browser extensions** do the heavy lifting:

- **Honey** – Applies every known code at checkout, instantly testing them for maximum savings.
- **Rakuten** – Offers coupon codes plus cash-back stacking, creating double savings.
- **Capital One Shopping** – Searches the web for valid promo codes and compares prices across retailers.
- **Cently** – Focuses on smaller and lesser-known coupon codes, giving you an edge over mainstream users.

These tools are particularly effective during Black Friday, when new codes are released hourly. While the average shopper applies one code, extensions may uncover **hidden or less-advertised discounts** most people never see.

Pro Tip: Use at least two extensions simultaneously. If one misses a code, the other may catch it.

1.4 Brand Newsletters & Email Exclusives

Retailers guard their **highest-value coupons** for email subscribers. These often include:

- **Welcome coupons** for new subscribers (10–25% off).
- **Early Black Friday codes** sent before the general public announcement.
- **Secret promotions** (e.g., "Take an extra 20% off clearance with this code").

The best strategy is to sign up for brand newsletters 3–4 weeks before Black Friday. This ensures you're on the mailing list just as retailers begin sending early access deals.

Pro Tip: Create a separate email folder (or filter) called "Black Friday Coupons." This organizes all incoming codes in one place for quick retrieval.

1.5 Cashback & Rebate Apps

Cashback platforms often double as coupon repositories:

- **Rakuten**, **Ibotta**, **TopCashback**, and **Dosh** not only apply coupons but also return a percentage of your purchase.
- On Black Friday, many apps **boost cashback rates** (sometimes from 5% to 15% or more), essentially turning your coupon into a double-discount weapon.

Pairing a retailer coupon with a boosted cashback offer is one of the most effective ways to maximize holiday savings.

1.6 Social Media & Deal Communities

Social platforms like **Reddit (r/deals, r/frugal, r/couponing)**, Facebook groups, and even TikTok creators are excellent sources for real-time coupon discoveries. Enthusiast communities often share:

- **Unadvertised stackable codes**.
- Flash deals spotted in retailer apps.
- Insider timing tips (such as "this code will expire in 2 hours" alerts).

The collaborative nature of these communities makes them invaluable during Black Friday, when deals appear and vanish within minutes.

Pro Tip: Join at least one community well before the event and set up mobile notifications. That way, you never miss limited-time coupon drops.

1.7 Credit Card & Banking Portals

Many people overlook **credit card reward portals**, yet they regularly contain high-value coupons tied to partnerships:

- **Amex Offers** and **Chase Offers** provide instant credits when you activate coupons through your online banking dashboard.
- These often include extra savings for retailers like Best Buy, Apple, and Amazon—major Black Friday players.

Pro Tip: Always check your credit card offers **before** making a purchase. Sometimes, activating a hidden coupon in your banking app can save you more than a public deal.

1.8 Insider & Employee Leaks

Finally, some of the most lucrative coupon codes come from **employee or insider leaks** shared online. While not always permanent, these codes can slash prices dramatically before being pulled. Communities like **Slickdeals** or private Discord servers are where these surface first.

Pro Tip: Use these codes quickly, as they are often time-sensitive and removed once retailers notice unusual redemption spikes.

Final Takeaway

Finding high-value digital coupons is not about luck—it's about **strategy and awareness**. By combining retailer programs, aggregators, extensions, newsletters, cashback apps, and community insights, you can build a **multi-layered couponing system**.

Chapter 2: Tools and Extensions That Do the Work for You

If Chapter 1 taught you *where* to find coupons, this chapter reveals *how to make them find you*. The modern couponer doesn't just scour websites manually; they harness **automation tools, browser extensions, and smart apps** that run quietly in the background, scanning for codes, testing them, and applying the best deal without lifting a finger.

During the high-speed chaos of Black Friday and Cyber Monday, these tools become indispensable. Time matters—prices fluctuate by the hour, codes expire in minutes, and checkout carts vanish when stock runs out. With automation in place, you'll gain the speed and accuracy needed to secure the lowest possible prices before others even realize the opportunity.

2.1 Honey – The Pioneer of Auto-Apply

Perhaps the most famous coupon extension, **Honey** (acquired by PayPal) transformed digital couponing by creating a simple, one-click system:

- At checkout, Honey automatically **tests dozens of coupon codes** for you.
- It then applies the **highest-value code** without you having to search.
- Its "Droplist" feature allows you to track items across stores, sending alerts when prices fall or new coupons become available.

Why It's a Must-Have: Honey shines on **Amazon**, where its price-tracking history reveals whether a Black Friday "deal" is truly a discount—or a cleverly disguised markup.

Pro Tip: Activate Honey's rewards program (Honey Gold). The points you accumulate can be redeemed as gift cards, adding another layer of hidden savings.

2.2 Rakuten – Double-Dip Discounts with Cashback

Rakuten (formerly Ebates) goes beyond coupons by combining them with **cashback offers**. The process is seamless:

1. Activate Rakuten before you shop.
2. The extension applies any available coupons.
3. You earn a percentage of your purchase back, often ranging from 2% to 15%.

During Black Friday, Rakuten frequently **boosts cashback rates**, sometimes doubling them for just 24 hours. This allows you to stack coupon savings with cash rewards, a strategy that compounds into major returns.

Pro Tip: Install the Rakuten browser extension rather than relying solely on the app. The extension pops up whenever a partnered retailer offers cashback, making it impossible to miss hidden opportunities.

2.3 Capital One Shopping – Price Comparison Master

While similar to Honey, **Capital One Shopping** excels at **real-time price comparison**. When you shop on sites like Amazon or Walmart, it scans thousands of other sellers to see if a lower price exists elsewhere.

- Automatically applies coupon codes at checkout.
- Alerts you if another retailer has the same product for less.
- Offers a rewards system that can be converted into gift cards.

Why It's Powerful: On Black Friday, when retailers strategically mark up "deals," this extension prevents you from being fooled. It gives you the **real price landscape** in seconds.

2.4 Cently – The Underdog Extension

Unlike big-name tools, **Cently** focuses on **smaller coupon databases**. While this means fewer codes overall, it often catches **niche deals** missed by competitors.

- Great for boutique shops and niche e-commerce brands.
- Automatically tests codes like other extensions but with different sources.
- Works well in combination with Honey or Capital One Shopping.

Pro Tip: Keep Cently installed as a backup. If your main extension misses a discount, Cently may catch the hidden gem.

2.5 Retailer-Specific Apps

Many stores now integrate coupon automation directly into their mobile apps:

- **Target Circle App** automatically applies available Target Circle deals at checkout.
- **Kohl's App** integrates Kohl's Cash and stackable coupon codes.
- **Best Buy App** frequently pushes limited-time codes to app users that never appear on the main site.

Why This Matters: Retailer apps often include **push notifications** that alert you to flash sales and coupons in real-time. On Black Friday, these alerts can be the difference between securing a deal and missing out.

2.6 Price-Tracking Tools Beyond Coupons

Automation isn't just about coupons—it's about knowing the **perfect moment to buy**. Tools like these expand your arsenal:

- **CamelCamelCamel** – Tracks Amazon price histories to expose false "discounts."
- **Keepa** – Offers in-depth price charts and alerts for Amazon, showing when an item historically hits its lowest price.
- **Honey Droplist** – Already mentioned in 2.1, but worth emphasizing as an integrated price tracker.

Pro Tip: Set alerts for high-ticket Black Friday items (TVs, laptops, gaming consoles) weeks in advance. If prices dip before Black Friday, you'll know whether to buy now or wait.

2.7 Mobile Wallets & Coupon Integrations

Apple Wallet and Google Wallet now support digital coupon storage, making it easier to keep all your deals in one place. Some retailers allow **direct barcode scanning from your phone**, eliminating the hassle of searching through apps at checkout.

- **Starbucks Rewards** integrates with Apple Wallet.
- **Walgreens** and **CVS** often allow digital coupon clipping straight into your mobile wallet.

This is particularly useful in-store on Black Friday, where speed matters at the checkout counter.

2.8 Automation Stacking Strategy

The real secret to maximizing these tools is not using just one, but **stacking them strategically**:

1. Use **Capital One Shopping** or **Honey** to apply coupons.
2. Activate **Rakuten** for cashback.
3. Layer with a **credit card offer** (covered in Chapter 1.7).
4. Apply retailer app coupons for bonus savings.

This creates a **multi-tiered savings system**, where every purchase works harder for you without extra effort.

Final Takeaway

Automation is the future of couponing. By leveraging tools like Honey, Rakuten, Capital One Shopping, and Cently—plus retailer apps and price trackers—you transform couponing from a time-consuming hobby into a **hands-free savings machine**.

When Black Friday hits, you won't scramble for codes. You'll glide through checkout, confident that your extensions are testing every option and applying the absolute best deal in seconds.

Chapter 3: Apps & Extensions That Organize Your Coupons Automatically

Finding and applying coupons is only half the battle. The other half is **organization**. A cluttered inbox, dozens of open browser tabs, and random promo codes scribbled on sticky notes can cause you to miss out on valuable deals when you need them most. The key to mastering Black Friday and Cyber Monday savings isn't just collecting coupons—it's knowing exactly where they are, how they stack, and when they expire.

Thankfully, technology has stepped in to eliminate the chaos. This chapter explores the **apps and extensions that automatically organize your coupons**, turning a messy system into a streamlined dashboard of ready-to-use savings. By the end, you'll be able to manage hundreds of coupons across multiple retailers without feeling overwhelmed.

3.1 The Case for Automated Organization

Couponing used to require a binder or accordion folder to keep track of expiration dates and categories. Digital couponing solved the paper problem, but it also created a new one: **information overload**. With retailers, cashback apps, newsletters, and browser extensions flooding you with codes, you risk missing the best deals simply because you can't keep them straight.

Automated coupon organization tools solve this problem by:

- **Collecting** coupons into one system.
- **Sorting** them by store, category, or expiration date.
- **Syncing** across devices so your desktop, tablet, and phone always match.
- **Applying** them in real time without manual searching.

3.2 Coupon-Organizing Apps

a. SnipSnap

- A popular app that lets you **save and digitize paper coupons** by snapping photos.
- Also integrates digital offers and organizes them into categories.
- Sends **expiration alerts** so you never miss a deadline.

Best Use Case: For hybrid couponers who still encounter printable or in-store paper coupons during the holiday rush.

b. CouponCabin

- A mix of cashback, coupon discovery, and organization.
- Coupons are saved inside the app, categorized by retailer.
- Offers **exclusive app-only codes** that won't appear on aggregator sites.

Best Use Case: When you want one app to handle **both discovery and organization** without juggling multiple platforms.

c. Ibotta

- Primarily known as a cashback app, but its interface also acts as a coupon wallet.
- Digital offers are clipped with one tap and linked to your loyalty cards.
- Scans receipts automatically to apply rewards.

Best Use Case: For grocery and household Black Friday deals, where loyalty program tie-ins maximize returns.

d. The Coupons App

- Stores thousands of digital coupons daily.
- Pushes **real-time alerts** when your saved coupons are about to expire.
- Organizes offers by **location**, useful for in-store Black Friday shopping.

Best Use Case: For shoppers who plan to blend **online and in-store deals** on Black Friday.

3.3 Browser Extensions with Built-In Organization

a. Honey's "Saved Coupons" Feature

- Beyond auto-applying, Honey also lets you **bookmark codes** for later.
- Useful for deals that don't activate until a specific date (common during Black Friday pre-sales).

b. Capital One Shopping's Price Tracking & Coupon Wallet

- Stores coupon codes tied to your account, accessible across devices.
- Integrates with its price comparison engine so you don't have to check multiple tabs.

c. RetailMeNot Deal Finder

- Saves your applied codes in a personal "wallet" for future purchases.
- Highlights **soon-to-expire codes** first, ensuring you prioritize maximum-value deals.

3.4 Email Management Tools

One of the biggest headaches in couponing is the flood of retailer emails. Instead of scrolling endlessly, use email-focused tools that act like a **coupon filter**:

- **Unroll.me** – Collects newsletters and compiles them into a daily digest, making coupon codes easier to spot.
- **Gmail Labels & Filters** – Create a "Coupons" label and filter all incoming promo emails into it.
- **Microsoft Outlook Rules** – Works similarly, organizing coupons automatically into a dedicated folder.

Pro Tip: Combine these with your coupon apps—when you get an email-exclusive coupon, drop it straight into SnipSnap or Honey's saved list.

3.5 Digital Wallet Integrations

Modern digital wallets (Apple Wallet, Google Wallet, Samsung Pay) are more than just payment tools. Many allow you to:

- **Save digital coupons and loyalty cards** in one swipe.
- Scan barcodes directly at checkout.
- Receive expiration alerts on your lock screen.

Best Use Case: For in-store Black Friday trips, where fumbling with apps could slow you down in long lines.

3.6 Building a Coupon Dashboard System

The most efficient couponers use multiple organization tools but connect them into a **single streamlined workflow**:

1. **Sign up for retailer newsletters** → Filter into a "Coupons" email folder.
2. **Clip coupons** into SnipSnap or Ibotta for easy mobile access.
3. **Enable extensions** like Honey or Capital One Shopping to apply codes automatically.
4. **Link loyalty cards** inside apps so coupons apply at checkout without scanning.
5. **Save high-value codes** into your mobile wallet for on-the-go use.

By combining these steps, you create a **living coupon dashboard**—a system where nothing slips through the cracks and every deal is ready when you are.

3.7 The Black Friday Advantage

Black Friday and Cyber Monday often involve dozens of purchases across different sites. Without organization, you'll lose track of:

- Which codes you've already used.
- Which offers expire first.
- Which retailers allow stacking.

By using automation-driven organization apps, you not only save more—you also **save time and mental energy**, freeing you to focus on choosing the right products instead of juggling codes.

Final Takeaway

The real masterclass in couponing isn't about collecting the most codes—it's about **organizing them into a system that works while you shop**. With apps like SnipSnap, Ibotta, and CouponCabin, browser extensions like Honey and Capital One Shopping, and email filters and wallet integrations, your coupons become as efficient as a digital filing cabinet.

No more expired codes. No more chaos. Just a streamlined arsenal of ready-to-fire savings tools.

Chapter 4: Secret Deal Forums and Communities

The world of digital couponing has a hidden layer that most casual shoppers never see. While apps and extensions are powerful, they only scratch the surface of what's possible. The *real magic* often happens in **forums, groups, and underground deal-sharing communities** where expert coupon hunters exchange codes, tips, and strategies that no algorithm will uncover.

These spaces are fast-paced, collaborative, and—during Black Friday—nothing short of electrifying. If you want to level up from automated savings to **elite coupon mastery**, you need to know where these forums are, how to use them effectively, and how to navigate the unspoken etiquette that keeps the best deals flowing.

4.1 Why Forums Matter

Apps like Honey or Rakuten rely on public databases of codes. Forums, on the other hand, are fueled by **real people in real time**:

- Users share **fresh codes** within minutes of discovery.
- Members post **stacking strategies** that combine multiple discounts into one massive win.
- Community-driven voting systems highlight the most valuable deals quickly.
- Some members leak **insider or employee-only coupons** before they hit mainstream outlets.

During Black Friday, these communities become gold mines of information—codes drop hourly, and the best ones often disappear just as fast.

4.2 Reddit: The Heart of Couponing Communities

Reddit is one of the most active spaces for coupon hunters. Key subreddits include:

- **r/deals** – General deals across all categories, updated constantly.
- **r/frugal** – Focused on long-term money-saving strategies, not just quick discounts.
- **r/couponing** – Dedicated to coupon stacking, printable deals, and digital codes.
- **r/buildapcsales** – If tech and electronics are on your Black Friday radar, this subreddit is legendary for real-time deal spotting.

Pro Tip: Subscribe to your preferred deal subreddits and enable notifications for hot posts. On Black Friday, these alerts can give you a critical head start before codes expire.

4.3 Slickdeals: The Deal Hunter's Playground

Slickdeals is more than a website—it's a community built entirely around saving money.

- Members submit coupons and deals, which are then voted on.
- Hot deals rise to the top, so you don't waste time on expired or low-value codes.
- The forum has specific sections for **Black Friday ads**, **coupon codes**, and **deal stacking techniques**.

What sets Slickdeals apart is its **collective intelligence**. Veteran deal hunters dissect sales, explaining how to combine retailer codes, gift card offers, and cashback portals for maximum impact.

4.4 Discord Servers & Private Groups

As couponing has gone digital, many deal hunters have migrated to **Discord servers, Telegram groups, and even private Facebook communities**. These invite-only spaces often contain:

- **Exclusive codes** not available anywhere else.
- Alerts for "price glitches" where items accidentally list too low.
- Tutorials on advanced stacking methods.
- Group-buys or shared bulk deals that lower prices even further.

Pro Tip: Start with larger public groups (Facebook deal communities or Discord "deal drops" channels) before moving into private circles. Building a reputation as a contributor will often earn you invites into the most valuable spaces.

4.5 Black Friday Ad Scan Communities

Some forums specialize in **leaked ad scans**, posting them weeks before retailers make them public. Sites like **BlackFriday.com** and **BFAds.net** often partner with community forums where members discuss how to pair these ads with coupon codes and cashback strategies.

This gives you a **planning advantage**, allowing you to create a coupon strategy before the sales even launch.

4.6 TikTok & Influencer Deals

It may sound unconventional, but TikTok and Instagram influencers have become major players in the couponing world. Many partner directly with retailers for **exclusive promo codes**, often shared only in their videos or captions.

- Search hashtags like **#BlackFridayDeals**, **#CouponingCommunity**, or **#DealHack**.
- Follow influencers known for **unboxing or haul videos**—they often slip in unique codes.

While less structured than forums, this can be a surprisingly rich source of **limited-use codes** designed to drive engagement.

4.7 How to Use Forums Effectively

Finding the right community is just the first step. To extract real value, follow these principles:

1. **Check Timestamps** – The fresher the post, the higher the chance the coupon still works.
2. **Read the Comments** – Other members often share stacking tricks or report whether a code is expired.
3. **Give Back** – Communities thrive on reciprocity. If you find a code or notice a glitch, post it.
4. **Stay Safe** – Avoid shady links. Stick to reputable sites or community-verified codes.

4.8 The Black Friday Advantage

During Black Friday, secret forums move at lightning speed:

- Retailers test codes in small batches before mass release. Communities catch them early.
- Members share **stacking formulas** like:
  Retailer coupon (20%) + Gift card promo + Cashback portal + Credit card offer.
- Codes sometimes vanish in less than an hour—forum alerts give you a chance to grab them before they're gone.

If apps and extensions are your autopilot, forums are your **insider playbook**—the difference between saving 20% and saving 60% on the same purchase.

Final Takeaway

Extensions like Honey and Rakuten are powerful, but they're limited by what's publicly available. Secret deal forums and communities are where coupon hunters graduate to the next level. These spaces unlock codes, leaks, and stacking strategies that no automated tool can replicate.

By participating in Reddit threads, Slickdeals discussions, Discord groups, and Black Friday ad forums, you step into a collective intelligence network that works 24/7 to uncover savings opportunities.

Chapter 5: Stacking Coupons with Store Sales

If finding coupons is the spark, **stacking them with store sales is the fire**. This is where casual couponing ends and true mastery begins. Retailers expect you to use one discount at a time—maybe a 20% off promo or a simple "$10 off $50" deal. But with the right timing, planning, and knowledge of store policies, you can **stack multiple offers together** so that every dollar saved multiplies into the kind of Black Friday wins that most shoppers don't believe are possible.

This chapter explores the **art and science of stacking**: how to combine store sales, coupons, loyalty rewards, and promotional events into a single purchase that maximizes every angle of savings.

5.1 What "Stacking" Means in Practice

In couponing, "stacking" means applying **more than one discount or reward** to the same purchase. While some retailers prohibit this, many allow it within specific guidelines. The trick is to know:

- **Which coupons can be combined** (store + manufacturer, digital + loyalty, promo code + cashback).
- **What order to apply them in** (some discounts must be added before others).
- **When stacking works best** (holiday sales, clearance events, bonus reward days).

Example: A $100 coat might already be 30% off in a Black Friday sale, bringing it down to $70. Add a 20% off store coupon, and it drops to $56. Pay with a credit card offering 10% cashback, and your final effective cost is just over $50. That's stacking in action.

5.2 Types of Coupons You Can Stack

Not all coupons are created equal. Understanding the categories helps you spot opportunities:

- **Store Coupons** – Issued by retailers (Target Circle, Kohl's Cash, Macy's promo codes).
- **Manufacturer Coupons** – Provided by product brands (common in groceries, beauty, and household goods).
- **Digital Coupons** – Loaded into your store account or app.
- **Loyalty Rewards** – Points, cash-back credits, or "spend $50, get $10" style promotions.
- **Gift Card Deals** – Retailers often run "Buy $100, get $20 gift card" promos around the holidays.

Key Principle: You can often **stack one manufacturer coupon + one store coupon + one sale price** on the same item. Add loyalty and gift card promos, and the savings compound dramatically.

5.3 Timing Sales for Maximum Stacking

The power of stacking comes not just from coupons, but from **when you use them**:

- **Pre-Black Friday Early Access** – Many stores drop coupons to lure customers in early. Stack these with storewide pre-sales before the big event.
- **Doorbusters** – Usually excluded from coupons, but sometimes stackable with loyalty rewards or credit card offers.
- **Clearance Markdowns** – After Christmas, clearance items are heavily discounted. If coupons are still valid, they can apply to already reduced prices.
- **Double/Triple Points Days** – Many loyalty programs multiply points during peak shopping days, effectively adding another layer of savings.

Pro Tip: Always read the fine print. Many coupons say "excludes Black Friday doorbusters" but still apply to other sale items.

5.4 Stacking Online vs. In-Store

Online Stacking

- Promo codes are entered at checkout.
- Browser extensions (Honey, Capital One Shopping) test available codes.
- Cashback portals like Rakuten can be layered on top.

In-Store Stacking

- Paper or digital coupons scanned at checkout.
- Store apps (Target Circle, Walgreens, Kohl's) apply offers automatically.
- Gift card deals are often **in-store only**, creating stacking opportunities not available online.

Hybrid Tip: Buy discounted gift cards online (through Raise or Rakuten's gift card promos), then use them in-store with coupons and loyalty rewards for triple-stack savings.

5.5 Stacking Strategies by Retailer

Target

- Combine **Target Circle offers** + **manufacturer coupons** + **weekly sales**.
- Add "Spend $50, get $10 Target gift card" promos for extra value.
- Best categories: groceries, household essentials, holiday décor.

Kohl's

- Famous for **Kohl's Cash stacking**.
- Typical formula: store coupon (20%) + clearance markdown + Kohl's Cash + Kohl's Rewards.
- Best categories: clothing, small kitchen appliances, Black Friday exclusives.

Walgreens / CVS

- Both allow **stacking store coupons** + **manufacturer coupons**.
- Rewards programs issue cash-like points (Walgreens Cash, ExtraBucks) that roll into future purchases.
- Best categories: beauty, personal care, over-the-counter meds.

Best Buy

- Limited coupon stacking, but strong **gift card promos**.
- Pair manufacturer rebates (on appliances/electronics) with store sales.
- Credit card offers (Amex, Chase) often double-dip here.

5.6 The Order of Operations

When stacking multiple discounts, the **order matters**. A simple formula looks like this:

1. **Apply storewide sale first** (Black Friday markdown).
2. **Apply store coupon** (e.g., 20% off).
3. **Apply manufacturer coupon** (often a flat dollar amount).
4. **Redeem loyalty rewards** (points, gift cards, cashback offers).
5. **Pay with a cashback credit card** (final layer of savings).

Example:

- Laptop marked down from $800 → $600 (store sale).
- Use 10% off store coupon → $540.
- Apply $50 manufacturer rebate → $490.
- Earn $40 store credit → $450 net.
- Pay with 5% cashback credit card → $427.50 effective cost.

5.7 Pitfalls to Avoid

- **Overlapping exclusions** – Some coupons cancel each other out if applied together.
- **Stacking beyond policy** – Forcing a cashier or system to override may cause issues. Stick to legit stacks.
- **Forgetting expiration dates** – Stacking only works if all discounts are valid at the same time.
- **Impulse stacking** – Don't buy items just because you *can* stack. The goal is value, not clutter.

5.8 The Black Friday Advantage

Stacking is especially powerful during Black Friday because:

- Retailers drop **short-term coupons** to push volume.
- Loyalty programs often offer **bonus points multipliers**.
- Cashback apps increase rates for the weekend.
- High-ticket items mean even a 5–10% extra stack equals massive dollar savings.

In other words, while most shoppers see "30% off Black Friday price," you'll be walking out with **50–70% off effective costs** by layering multiple discounts.

Final Takeaway

Stacking coupons with store sales is where you stop being a coupon collector and become a **savings strategist**. By combining store coupons, manufacturer discounts, loyalty rewards, gift card promos, and cashback opportunities, you create a compounding effect that turns good deals into extraordinary ones.

Chapter 6: Cash-Back Sites & Rebate Combos

If stacking coupons and store sales is the foundation of savings, **cash-back sites and rebates are the secret reinforcements** that push your discounts into uncharted territory. Most shoppers think they've done well with a 20% coupon, but the real pros know you can **earn money back** even after applying every other discount.

In this chapter, we'll explore how cash-back sites, apps, and rebate systems work, and how to combine them with store sales, loyalty programs, and coupons for multi-layered wins.

6.1 What Is Cash-Back Shopping?

Cash-back shopping is simple in concept but powerful in practice:

1. You start your shopping trip through a **cash-back portal or app**.
2. That portal earns a commission from the retailer for sending traffic.
3. Instead of keeping the commission, the portal **shares part of it with you** as cash back.

The result? Extra savings layered on top of every coupon, sale, and promo code you've already applied.

6.2 Top Cash-Back Sites

Rakuten

- The most well-known portal (formerly Ebates).
- Offers cash back at **3,500+ stores** including Walmart, Target, Best Buy, and Macy's.
- Frequently runs **double or triple cash-back events** during Black Friday and Cyber Monday.

TopCashback

- Known for higher-than-average payout percentages.
- Often edges out Rakuten by 1–2% at the same store.
- Offers both cash payouts and gift card redemptions.

BeFrugal

- A rising competitor that aggressively matches or beats other portals.
- Includes **sign-up bonuses** for new users.

Mr. Rebates

- One of the oldest portals.
- Simple interface, reliable payouts, and strong **holiday bonus offers**.

Pro Tip: Create accounts at multiple cash-back sites. Use comparison tools (like Cashback Monitor) to check which portal has the highest rate before every Black Friday purchase.

6.3 Cash-Back Apps

Ibotta

- Popular for groceries, but expanding into retail and Black Friday deals.
- Offers **instant cash-back rewards** by linking loyalty cards or scanning receipts.

Dosh

- Automatic cash-back when you use a linked credit card at participating retailers.
- No need to activate offers manually.

Drop

- Rewards points for shopping through the app, redeemable for gift cards.
- Often partners with Black Friday brands like Amazon, Uber, and Sephora.

Shopkick

- Unique in that you earn "kicks" not only for purchases but also for **scanning products in-store**.
- Great for hybrid Black Friday shopping (online + physical store trips).

6.4 Rebates: Old-School Meets Digital

Rebates once meant mailing in forms and waiting 6–8 weeks for a check. Today, most are **instant or digital**:

- **Manufacturer Rebates** – Common with electronics and appliances. Example: LG offering $100 back on TVs purchased during Black Friday.
- **Store Rebates** – Best Buy, Staples, and Home Depot often run rebate programs layered onto store sales.
- **Credit Card Rebates** – Amex, Chase, and Capital One frequently offer "spend $X, get $Y back" promotions through their online portals.

Pro Tip: Always check if your Black Friday electronics purchases include a rebate. Big-ticket rebates can turn a great deal into a once-in-a-lifetime steal.

6.5 Stacking Cash-Back with Coupons

Here's how a **layered transaction** might look in action:

1. Start your purchase through Rakuten (10% cash back).
2. Use a 20% store coupon.
3. Apply a $50 manufacturer rebate.
4. Pay with a 5% cash-back credit card.

Result: You've applied every savings layer possible: store coupon, rebate, portal, and card. The final effective cost could be **40–60% less** than the listed price.

6.6 Timing Black Friday Cash-Back Boosts

During Black Friday and Cyber Monday, cash-back sites often compete for traffic by **supercharging their rates**:

- A retailer that normally pays 2% cash back may jump to 10–15%.
- Many sites run **hourly flash boosts** where rates spike temporarily.
- Some portals offer **stackable gift card bonuses** if you redeem your cash back as store credit instead of cash.

Pro Tip: Bookmark your favorite cash-back sites and check their Black Friday pages daily—especially in the days leading up to Cyber Monday.

6.7 Common Mistakes to Avoid

- **Forgetting to activate the portal:** You must start your shopping trip from the cash-back site, or it won't track.
- **Using multiple portals at once:** Only one can earn commission per purchase.
- **Ad blockers interfering:** Disable ad blockers during checkout to ensure cash-back tracking.
- **Ignoring payout thresholds:** Some sites require $20+ before you can cash out.

6.8 Case Example

Let's break down a **realistic Black Friday stack** on a $500 electronics purchase:

- **Retailer Sale:** $500 TV marked down to $400.
- **Store Coupon:** Extra 10% off → $360.
- **Manufacturer Rebate:** $50 mail-in rebate → $310.
- **Rakuten Cash Back:** 12% → $43.20 returned.
- **Credit Card Cash Back:** 5% → $15 back.

Final Effective Cost: $251.80 — almost **half off the Black Friday price** most shoppers stopped at.

6.9 Building a Rebate & Cash-Back Routine

1. **Check portals first.** Before buying, see which has the best rate.
2. **Activate cash-back extensions.** Let them remind you at checkout.
3. **Pair with coupons.** Apply store or manufacturer codes before finalizing.
4. **Claim rebates immediately.** Submit online forms the same day—don't let procrastination steal your savings.
5. **Track payouts.** Create a spreadsheet or use apps that notify you when rebates post.

Final Takeaway

Cash-back sites and rebates turn every purchase into an **income-generating opportunity**, transforming the way you shop. When layered with coupons, store sales, and loyalty rewards, they push savings into the extraordinary.

Chapter 7: Real-Life Case Studies of Coupon Wins

Theory gives you the tools. Real-life stories show you how those tools come alive. In this chapter, we'll explore case studies that demonstrate exactly how coupon hunters—ordinary shoppers with extraordinary strategies—turned Black Friday and Cyber Monday into opportunities for massive savings. Each case illustrates a different **stacking strategy**, combining store sales, coupons, cash-back portals, and rebate systems.

These stories will show you what's possible when you combine persistence, organization, and timing with the methods we've covered so far.

7.1 The Tech Enthusiast's Dream TV

Scenario:

Marcus, a college student, wanted a 65-inch 4K Smart TV listed at **$899** for Black Friday. His budget was tight, but he was determined to squeeze every dollar.

Strategy:

1. Found the TV in a Black Friday ad scan, marked down to **$699**.
2. Used a store-wide coupon from Best Buy (10% off electronics) → **$629.10**.
3. Discovered a **$50 manufacturer rebate** valid during the holiday weekend → **$579.10**.
4. Started the purchase through **Rakuten (12% cash back)** → **$69.49** back.
5. Paid with a **5% cash-back credit card** → **$31.45** back.

Final Effective Cost: $478.16

Savings: Over **$420** off retail. Marcus stacked a store sale, a store coupon, a manufacturer rebate, Rakuten, and his credit card to cut the price nearly in half.

7.2 The Grocery Warrior's Holiday Stock-Up

Scenario:

Linda, a mother of three, wanted to stretch her budget by stocking up on holiday essentials during Black Friday grocery promotions.

Strategy:

1. Clipped **digital coupons** in her Kroger app: $10 off $50 + $1.50 off each butter purchase.
2. Used a **manufacturer coupon** for baking flour: $2 off per bag.
3. Took advantage of a **"Spend $100, Get $20 Kroger Cash"** promotion.
4. Scanned her receipts into **Ibotta**, earning $15 in rebates on dairy, baking goods, and snacks.
5. Paid with her **grocery rewards credit card (6% cash back)**.

Final Effective Cost: She spent $120 in-store, but after coupons, store cash, rebates, and cash back, her net cost was **$72**.

Savings: Nearly **40% off** her entire holiday grocery haul.

7.3 The Fashion Shopper's Winter Wardrobe

Scenario:

Tara wanted to refresh her winter wardrobe—coats, sweaters, and boots. She targeted Kohl's Black Friday deals.

Strategy:

1. Shopped during Kohl's **50% off Black Friday markdowns**.
2. Applied a **20% off store coupon** (valid online and in-store).
3. Earned **$15 Kohl's Cash per $50 spent** (a typical Black Friday promo).
4. Started her order through **TopCashback (10%)**.
5. Paid with Kohl's Rewards Visa, adding an extra **7.5% back** in store rewards.

Final Effective Cost:

- Original total: $400.
- Black Friday sale → $200.
- Coupon → $160.
- Earned $45 Kohl's Cash + $12 store rewards + $16 TopCashback.

Her final effective spend: **$87**.

Savings: Over **$310** in value, plus future Kohl's Cash for another purchase.

7.4 The Gamer's Console Bundle

Scenario:

James wanted a new gaming console bundle advertised at $499, including two games.

Strategy:

1. Started purchase via **BeFrugal (8% cash back)**.
2. Applied a limited-time **$50 off digital coupon** shared in a Discord deal forum.
3. Took advantage of a **store promo: Buy console, get $50 gift card**.
4. Paid with a credit card that had a **holiday promo: Spend $500, earn $75 back**.

Final Effective Cost:

- Original bundle: $499.
- Coupon: $449.
- Cash back: $35.92.
- Gift card: $50.
- Credit card rebate: $75.

Net cost after all rewards: $288.08.

Savings: Over **$210** plus a free $50 gift card for a future purchase.

7.5 The Small Business Owner's Office Supplies

Scenario:

Ellen, who runs a small home business, needed to stock up on ink, paper, and office supplies before tax season.

Strategy:

1. Purchased during Staples' **Black Friday 50% off supply sale**.
2. Applied a **20% off coupon code** from RetailMeNot.
3. Used a **"Spend $75, Get $15 Staples Rewards"** promotion.
4. Claimed a **$20 manufacturer rebate** on printer ink.
5. Routed her order through **Mr. Rebates (6%)**.

Final Effective Cost:

- Original spend: $200.
- Sale + coupon: $80 saved → $120.
- Staples Rewards: $15 credit.
- Rebate: $20.
- Cash back: $7.20.

Net cost: $77.80.

Savings: More than **60% off** needed supplies.

7.6 Key Lessons Across Case Studies

1. **Stacking multiplies results.** Every layer matters—one coupon might save you 20%, but combining five strategies turns that into 50–70% off.
2. **Timing is everything.** The biggest wins came when shoppers used cash-back boosts, short-term coupons, or loyalty multipliers specific to Black Friday.
3. **Communities unlock hidden codes.** James' console deal only worked because he belonged to a Discord forum that posted the $50 code before it hit mainstream.
4. **Rewards are part of the equation.** Future credits (Kohl's Cash, Staples Rewards) aren't just "extra"—they're part of the long game of continuous savings.

Final Takeaway

Real-life case studies prove that digital couponing isn't theory—it's a practical system that transforms the way you shop. By combining the strategies from previous chapters—automation, forums, organization, stacking, cash-back, and rebates—you can create results that feel almost unfair.

While most shoppers think Black Friday deals are already as good as it gets, you now know the truth: the **real discounts begin when you apply coupon mastery to the sales everyone else accepts at face value**.

Appendix A: Coupon App Comparison Chart

When you're juggling dozens of coupon sources, it helps to know exactly what each app brings to the table. Not all coupon apps are created equal—some specialize in groceries, others excel in stacking cash-back, and some shine during holiday shopping sprees. This appendix provides a side-by-side comparison of the most popular and powerful coupon apps so you can build your personalized **coupon toolkit**.

1. Quick-Glance Comparison Table

App Name	Best For	Coupon Types	Extra Features	Strengths	Limitations
Rakuten	General Black Friday shopping, big retailers	Promo codes + automatic cash back	Browser extension, double cash-back events	High cash-back rates, easy payouts	Only works if you start purchase through Rakuten
Honey	Online shopping at multiple stores	Auto-applied promo codes	Droplist (price tracking), Honey Gold rewards	Hands-off, applies best code instantly	Doesn't cover every retailer
Capital One Shopping	Price comparison + coupon application	Promo codes	Price tracking, gift card redemption	Excellent for Amazon & electronics	Rewards system limited to gift cards

App Name	Best For	Coupon Types	Extra Features	Strengths	Limitations
Snip-Snap	Converting paper coupons to digital	Scanned paper + store coupons	Expiration reminders	Bridges paper + digital worlds	Less effective for online-only shopping
Ibotta	Grocery + household shopping	Digital store coupons + rebates	Receipt scanning, loyalty card linking	Real cash payouts	More time-intensive (requires scanning)
CouponCabin	All-around savings across retailers	Coupons + cash-back	App-only codes, cash-back tracking	Strong for seasonal promos	Slightly smaller database than Rakuten
Dosh	In-store purchases with linked cards	Automatic rebates	No activation needed	Passive savings	Limited merchant network
Shop-kick	Hybrid online + in-store	Store offers, gift cards	Earn "kicks" by scanning items	Fun gamified approach	Slower to accumulate rewards

App Name	Best For	Coupon Types	Extra Features	Strengths	Limitations
BeFrugal	Competing with Rakuten + TopCashback	Coupons + cash-back	Higher cash-back guarantees	High payout rates	Less polished app design

2. Detailed App Profiles

Rakuten

- **Best Feature:** Double cash-back events during Black Friday and Cyber Monday.
- **Payouts:** Quarterly via PayPal or check.
- **Standout Use Case:** Buying electronics and home goods online during holiday sales.

Honey

- **Best Feature:** Tests multiple coupon codes instantly at checkout.
- **Payouts:** Honey Gold points redeemable as gift cards.
- **Standout Use Case:** Amazon shopping—reveals price history to confirm real discounts.

Capital One Shopping

- **Best Feature:** Price comparison across thousands of retailers.
- **Payouts:** Rewards redeemable as gift cards.
- **Standout Use Case:** Big-ticket items like laptops, where price matching matters.

SnipSnap

- **Best Feature:** Turns any paper coupon into a digital version with one snap.
- **Payouts:** Not applicable (savings applied directly).
- **Standout Use Case:** Hybrid shoppers who combine in-store paper deals with digital couponing.

Ibotta

- **Best Feature:** Scan receipts to earn instant rebates.
- **Payouts:** PayPal, Venmo, or gift cards.
- **Standout Use Case:** Holiday grocery and baking supply shopping.

CouponCabin

- **Best Feature:** Cash-back + exclusive app-only coupons.
- **Payouts:** PayPal, check, or gift card.
- **Standout Use Case:** Apparel and seasonal shopping during Black Friday.

Dosh

- **Best Feature:** Automatic rebates linked to your credit/debit card.
- **Payouts:** Direct bank deposit, Venmo, PayPal.
- **Standout Use Case:** In-store Black Friday shopping—savings without scanning.

Shopkick

- **Best Feature:** Earn rewards ("kicks") just for walking into stores or scanning products.
- **Payouts:** Gift cards only.
- **Standout Use Case:** Blended shopping trips where you're visiting both online and physical stores.

BeFrugal

- **Best Feature:** Higher-than-average cash-back rates.
- **Payouts:** PayPal, check, gift cards.
- **Standout Use Case:** Price-conscious shoppers who compare multiple cash-back portals before every purchase.

3. Choosing the Right App for You

- **If you want automation and simplicity:** Start with **Honey + Rakuten**.
- **If you're focused on groceries/household items:** Add **Ibotta**.
- **If you shop heavily in-store:** Consider **SnipSnap** and **Dosh**.
- **If you want maximum rates across portals:** Compare **Rakuten, TopCashback, and BeFrugal** before each purchase.
- **If you enjoy gamified savings:** Try **Shopkick** for extra rewards just by scanning items.

4. Power Stacks

Apps are powerful alone, but combined, they become unstoppable:

- **Honey + Rakuten + Credit Card Cash Back** → Online shopping triple stack.
- **Ibotta + Store Loyalty Card + Manufacturer Coupon** → Grocery powerhouse stack.
- **SnipSnap + Dosh + Store Promo** → In-store Black Friday advantage.

Final Takeaway

No single app dominates every category of couponing. The secret is creating a **balanced toolkit**—a few apps for automation, a few for cashback, and a few for organizing and stacking. By mixing and matching based on your shopping habits, you'll never leave savings on the table.

Appendix B: Coupon Stacking Strategy

Most people stop at one coupon and feel they've "won." But the real savings happen when you **stack multiple layers of discounts together**. The trick is knowing what order to do things in, which discounts can combine, and how to make sure nothing slips through the cracks.

This appendix breaks down stacking as a simple, repeatable strategy anyone can follow.

Step 1: Start With the Sale Price

Always begin with what the store is offering first:

- Black Friday markdowns
- Clearance reductions
- Buy-One-Get-One offers

◈ *Example:* A winter coat originally $120 is marked down to $80 for Black Friday. That $80 becomes your starting point.

Step 2: Add a Store Coupon

Next, layer a **store coupon** (the kind issued by Target, Kohl's, Macy's, etc.).

- These are often percentage discounts (like 20% off) or fixed-dollar offers ($10 off $50).
- They stack on top of the sale price.

◈ *Example:* $80 coat – 20% off store coupon = $64.

Step 3: Add a Manufacturer Coupon (If Available)

Manufacturer coupons are provided by the brand itself (like Kellogg's for cereal or LG for electronics).

- These often give flat discounts, such as $5 or $50 off specific items.
- Many retailers allow **one store coupon + one manufacturer coupon** on the same product.

🔍 *Example:* $64 coat – $10 manufacturer coupon = $54.

Step 4: Factor in Loyalty Rewards or Store Cash

Most big retailers have a rewards system:

- **Target Circle, Walgreens Cash, CVS ExtraBucks, Kohl's Cash.**
- These usually give you credit for future purchases, but they still reduce your *effective* cost.

🔍 *Example:* $54 coat earns $10 Kohl's Cash → real cost drops to $44 when you count the store credit.

Step 5: Activate a Cash-Back Portal or App

Before checking out online, **always start your shopping trip through a cash-back site** like Rakuten, TopCashback, or BeFrugal. For in-store, use apps like Ibotta or Dosh.

- Cash-back portals pay you a percentage of your total back after the purchase.
- This is layered on top of all other coupons and rewards.

⟐ *Example:* $44 coat purchased through Rakuten with 10% cash back = $4.40 back. Final cost = $39.60.

Step 6: Use a Cash-Back Credit Card

Finally, pay with a credit card that offers rewards:

- 3–6% back on groceries, 5% back on Amazon, or seasonal holiday promos.
- These rewards apply on top of everything else.

⟐ *Example:* $39.60 coat paid with a 5% cash-back card = $1.98 back. Final effective cost = **$37.62.**

Putting It All Together (Simple Formula)

1. **Start with the sale price.**
2. **Apply a store coupon.**
3. **Apply a manufacturer coupon.**
4. **Collect loyalty/store rewards.**
5. **Shop through a cash-back site or app.**
6. **Pay with a cash-back credit card.**

Every step shaves off a little more until your deal is as low as it can possibly go.

Bonus Tips for Everyday Shoppers

- **Don't skip rewards credits.** Even if they're for future use, they're money in your pocket.
- **Check exclusions.** Doorbusters and clearance items sometimes exclude coupons, but often still count for loyalty rewards or cash back.
- **Time it right.** The best stacks happen during bonus multiplier days (double cash back, double points, holiday promos).
- **Always submit rebates right away.** Don't let procrastination erase a layer of your savings.

Final Takeaway

Think of stacking like building a sandwich: each ingredient adds flavor, and together they create something far more satisfying than a single slice of bread. By layering sales, coupons, rewards, cash-back, and rebates, you can transform everyday purchases into **deep discounts most shoppers never achieve**.

This isn't extreme couponing—it's **smart shopping strategy**. With practice, it becomes second nature, and soon you'll start looking at every purchase and asking, *"How many layers can I stack on this?"*

Message from the Author:

I hope you enjoyed this book, I love astrology and knew there was not a book such as this out on the shelf. I love metaphysical items as well. Please check out my other books:

-Life of Government Benefits

-My life of Hell

-My life with Hydrocephalus

-Red Sky

-World Domination:Woman's rule

-World Domination:Woman's Rule 2: The War

-Life and Banishment of Apophis: book 1

-The Kidney Friendly Diet

-The Ultimate Hemp Cookbook

-Creating a Dispensary(legally)

-Cleanliness throughout life: the importance of showering from childhood to adulthood.

-Strong Roots: The Risks of Overcoddling children

-Hemp Horoscopes: Cosmic Insights and Earthly Healing

- Celestial Hemp Navigating the Zodiac: Through the Green Cosmos

-Astrological Hemp: Aligning The Stars with Earth's Ancient Herb

-The Astrological Guide to Hemp: Stars, Signs, and Sacred Leaves

-Green Growth: Innovative Marketing Strategies for your Hemp Products and Dispensary

-Cosmic Cannabis

-Astrological Munchies

-Henry The Hemp

-Zodiacal Roots: The Astrological Soul Of Hemp

- **Green Constellations: Intersection of Hemp and Zodiac**

-Hemp in The Houses: An astrological Adventure Through The Cannabis Galaxy

-Galactic Ganja Guide

Heavenly Hemp
Zodiac Leaves
Doctor Who Astrology
Cannastrology
Stellar Satvias and Cosmic Indicas
Celestial Cannabis: A Zodiac Journey
AstroHerbology: The Sky and The Soil: Volume 1
AstroHerbology:Celestial Cannabis:Volume 2
Cosmic Cannabis Cultivation
The Starry Guide to Herbal Harmony: Volume 1
The Starry Guide to Herbal Harmony: Cannabis Universe: Volume 2
Yugioh Astrology: Astrological Guide to Deck, Duels and more
Nightmare Mansion: Echoes of The Abyss
Nightmare Mansion 2: Legacy of Shadows
Nightmare Mansion 3: Shadows of the Forgotten
Nightmare Mansion 4: Echoes of the Damned
The Life and Banishment of Apophis: Book 2
Nightmare Mansion: Halls of Despair
Healing with Herb: Cannabis and Hydrocephalus
Planetary Pot: Aligning with Astrological Herbs: Volume 1
Fast Track to Freedom: 30 Days to Financial Independence Using AI, Assets, and Agile Hustles
Cosmic Hemp Pathways
How to Become Financially Free in 30 Days: 10,000 Paths to Prosperity
Zodiacal Herbage: Astrological Insights: Volume 1
Nightmare Mansion: Whispers in the Walls
The Daleks Invade Atlantis
Henry the hemp and Hydrocephalus

10X The Kidney Friendly Diet
Cannabis Universe: Adult coloring book

Hemp Astrology: The Healing Power of the Stars

Zodiacal Herbage: Astrological Insights: Cannabis Universe: Volume 2

Planetary Pot: Aligning with Astrological Herbs: Cannabis Universes: Volume 2

Doctor Who: Convergence Protocol – The Replicator War

Nightmare Mansion: Curse of the Blood Moon

The Celestial Stoner: A Guide to the Zodiac

Cosmic Pleasures: Sex Toy Astrology for Every Sign

Hydrocephalus Astrology: Navigating the Stars and Healing Waters

Lapis and the Mischievous Chocolate Bar

Celestial Positions: Sexual Astrology for Every Sign

Apophis's Shadow Work Journal: : A Journey of Self-Discovery and Healing

Kinky Cosmos: Sexual Kink Astrology for Every Sign

Digital Cosmos: The Astrological Digimon Compendium

Stellar Seeds: The Cosmic Guide to Growing with Astrology

Apophis's Daily Gratitude Journal

Cat Astrology: Feline Mysteries of the Cosmos

The Cosmic Kama Sutra: An Astrological Guide to Sexual Positions

Unleash Your Potential: A Guided Journal Powered by AI Insights

Whispers of the Enchanted Grove

Cosmic Pleasures: An Astrological Guide to Sexual Kinks

369, 12 Manifestation Journal

Whisper of the nocturne journal(blank journal for writing or drawing)

The Boogey Book

Locked In Reflection: A Chastity Journey Through Locktober

Generating Wealth Quickly:How to Generate $100,000 in 24 Hours

Star Magic: Harness the Power of the Universe

The Flatulence Chronicles: A Fart Journal for Self-Discovery

The Doctor and The Death Moth

Seize the Day: A Personal Seizure Tracking Journal

The Ultimate Boogeyman Safari: A Journey into the Boogie World and Beyond

Whispers of Samhain: 1,000 Spells of Love, Luck, and Lunar Magic: Samhain Spell Book

Apophis's guides:Witch's Spellbook Crafting Guide for Halloween

Frost & Flame: The Enchanted Yule Grimoire of 1000 Winter Spells

The Ultimate Boogey Goo Guide & Spooky Activities for Halloween Fun

Harmony of the Scales: A Libra's Spellcraft for Balance and Beauty

The Enchanted Advent: 36 Days of Christmas Wonders

Nightmare Mansion: The Labyrinth of Screams

Harvest of Enchantment: 1,000 Spells of Gratitude, Love, and Fortune for Thanksgiving

The Boogey Chronicles: A Journal of Nightly Encounters and Shadowy Secrets

The 12 Days of Financial Freedom: A Step-by-Step Christmas Countdown to Transform Your Finances

Sigil of the Eternal Spiral Blank Journal

A Christmas Feast: Timeless Recipes for Every Meal

Holiday Stress-Free Solutions: A Survival Guide to Thriving During the Festive Season

Yu-Gi-Oh! Holiday Gifting Mastery: The Ultimate Guide for Fans and Newcomers Alike

Holiday Harmony: A Hydrocephalus Survival Guide for the Festive Season

Celestial Craft: The Witch's Almanac for 2025 – A Cosmic Guide to Manifestations, Moons, and Mystical Events

Doctor Who: The Toymaker's Winter Wonderland

Tulsa King Unveiled: A Thrilling Guide to Stallone's Mafia Masterpiece

Pendulum Craft: A Complete Guide to Crafting and Using Personalized Divination Tools

Nightmare Mansion: Santa's Eternal Eve

Starlight Noel: A Cosmic Journey through Christmas Mysteries

The Dark Architect: Unlocking the Blueprint of Existence

Surviving the Embrace: The Ultimate Guide to Encounters with The Hugging Molly

The Enchanted Codex: Secrets of the Craft for Witches, Wiccans, and Pagans

Harvest of Gratitude: A Complete Thanksgiving Guide

Yuletide Essentials: A Complete Guide to an Authentic and Magical Christmas

Celestial Smokes: A Cosmic Guide to Cigars and Astrology

Living in Balance: A Comprehensive Survival Guide to Thriving with Diabetes Insipidus

Cosmic Symbiosis: The Venom Zodiac Chronicles

The Cursed Paw of Ambition

Cosmic Symbiosis: The Astrological Venom Journal

Celestial Wonders Unfold: A Stargazer's Guide to the Cosmos (2024-2029)

The Ultimate Black Friday Prepper's Guide: Mastering Shopping Strategies and Savings

Cosmic Sales: The Astrological Guide to Black Friday Shopping

Legends of the Corn Mother and Other Harvest Myths

Whispers of the Harvest: The Corn Mother's Journal

The Evergreen Spellbook

The Doctor Meets the Boogeyman

The White Witch of Rose Hall's SpellBook

The Gingerbread Golem's Shadow: A Study in Sweet Darkness

The Gingerbread Golem Codex: An Academic Exploration of Sweet Myths

The Gingerbread Golem Grimoire: Sweet Magicks and Spells for the Festive Witch

The Curse of the Gingerbread Golem

10-minute Christmas Crafts for kids

Christmas Crisis Solutions: The Ultimate Last-Minute Survival Guide

Gingerbread Golem Recipes: Holiday Treats with a Magical Twist

The Infinite Key: Unlocking Mystical Secrets of the Ages

Enchanted Yule: A Wiccan and Pagan Guide to a Magical and Memorable Season

Dinosaurs of Power: Unlocking Ancient Magick

Astro-Dinos: The Cosmic Guide to Prehistoric Wisdom

Gallifrey's Yule Logs: A Festive Doctor Who Cookbook

The Dino Grimoire: Secrets of Prehistoric Magick

The Gift They Never Knew They Needed

The Gingerbread Golem's Culinary Alchemy: Enchanting Recipes for a Sweetly Dark Feast

A Time Lord Christmas: Holiday Adventures with the Doctor

Krampusproofing Your Home: Defensive Strategies for Yule

Silent Frights: A Collection of Christmas Creepypastas to Chill Your Bones

Santa Raptor's Jolly Carnage: A Dino-Claus Christmas Tale

Prehistoric Palettes: A Dino Wicca Coloring Journey

The Christmas Wishkeeper Chronicles

The Starlight Sleigh: A Holiday Journey

Elf Secrets: The True Magic of the North Pole

Candy Cane Conjurations

Cooking with Kids: Recipes Under 20 Minutes

Doctor Who: The TARDIS Confiscation

The Anxiety First Aid Kit: Quick Tools to Calm Your Mind

Frosty Whispers: A Winter's Tale

The Infinite Key: Unlocking the Secrets to Prosperity, Resilience, and Purpose

The Grasping Void: Why You'll Regret This Purchase

Astrology for Busy Bees: Star Signs Simplified

The Instant Focus Formula: Cut Through the Noise

The Secret Language of Colors: Unlocking the Emotional Codes

Sacred Fossil Chronicles: Blank Journal

The Christmas Cottage Miracle

Feeding Frenzy: Graboid-Inspired Recipes

Manifest in Minutes: The Quick Law of Attraction Guide

The Symbiote Chronicles: Doctor Who's Venomous Journey

Think Tiny, Grow Big: The Minimalist Mindset

The Energy Key: Unlocking Limitless Motivation

New Year, New Magic: Manifesting Your Best Year Yet

Unstoppable You: Mastering Confidence in Minutes

Infinite Energy: The Secret to Never Feeling Drained

Lightning Focus: Mastering the Art of Productivity in a Distracted World

Saturnalia Manifestation Magick: A Guide to Unlocking Abundance During the Solstice

Graboids and Garland: The Ultimate Tremors-Themed Christmas Guide

12 Nights of Holiday Magic

The Power of Pause: 60-Second Mindfulness Practices

The Quick Reset: How to Reclaim Your Life After Burnout

The Shadow Eater: A Tale of Despair and Survival

The Micro-Mastery Method: Transform Your Skills in Just Minutes a Day

Reclaiming Time: How to Live More by Doing Less

Chronovore: The Eternal Nexus

The Mind Reset: Unlocking Your Inner Peace in a Chaotic World
Confidence Code: Building Unshakable Self-Belief
Baby the Vampire Terrier
Baby the Vampire Terrier's Christmas Adventure
Celestial Streams: The Content Creator's Astrology Manual
The Wealth Whisperer: Unlocking Abundance with Everyday Actions
The Energy Equation: Maximize Your Output Without Burning Out
The Happiness Algorithm: Science-Backed Steps to Joyful Living
Stress-Free Success: Achieving Goals Without Anxiety
Mindful Wealth: The New Blueprint for Financial Freedom
The Festive Flavors of New Year: A Culinary Celebration
The Master's Gambit: Keys of Eternal Power
Shadowed Secrets: Groundhog Day Mysteries
Beneath the Burrow: Lessons from the Groundhog
Spring's Whispers: The Groundhog's Prediction
The Limitless Mindset: Unlock Your Untapped Potential
The Focus Funnel: How to Cut Through Chaos and Get Results
Bold Moves: Building Courage to Live on Your Terms
The Daily Shift: Simple Practices for Lasting Transformation
The Quarter-Life Reset: Thriving in Your 20s and 30s
The Art of Shadowplay: Building Your Own Personal Myth
The Eternal Loop: Finding Purpose in Repetition
Burrowing Wisdom: Life Lessons from the Groundhog
Shadow Work: A Groundhog Day Perspective
Love in Bloom: 5-Minute Romantic Gestures
The Shadowspell Codex: Secrets of Forbidden Magick
The Burnout Cure: Finding Balance in a Busy World
The Groundhog Prophecy: Unlocking Seasonal Secrets
Nog Tales: The Spirited History of Eggnog
Six More Weeks: Embracing Seasonal Transitions
The Lumivian Chronicles: Fragments of the Fifth Dimension

Money on Your Mind: A Beginner's Guide to Wealth
The Focus Fix: Breaking Through Distraction
January's Spirit Keepers: Mystical Protectors of the Cold
Creativity Unchained: Unlocking Your Wildest Ideas in 2025
Manifestation Mastery: 365 Days to Rewrite Your Reality
The Groundhog's Mirror: Reflecting on Change
The Weeping Angels' Christmas Curse
Burrowed in Time: A Groundhog Day Journey
Heartbeats: Poems to Share with Your Valentine
Dino Wicca: The Sacred Grimoire of Prehistoric Magick
Courage of the Pride: Finding Your Inner Roar
The Lion's Leap: Bold Moves for Big Results
Healthy Hustle: Achieving Without Overworking
Practical Manifesting: Turning Dreams into Reality in 2025
Jurassic Pharaohs: Unlocking the Magick of Ancient Egypt and Dino Wicca
The Happiness Equation: Small Changes for Big Joy
The Confidence Compass: Finding Your Inner Strength
Whispers in the Hollow: Tales of the Forgotten Beasts
Echoes from the Hollow: The Return of Forgotten Beasts
The Hollow Ascendant: The Rise of the Forgotten Beasts
The Relationship Reset: Building Better Connections
Mastering the Morning: How to Win the Day Before 8 AM
The Shadow's Dance: Groundhog Day Symbolism
Cupid's Kitchen: Quick Valentine's Day Recipes
Valentine's Day on a Budget: Love Without Breaking the Bank
Astrocraft: Aligning the Stars in the World of Minecraft
Forecasting Life: Groundhog Day Reflections
Bleeding Hearts: Twisted Tales of Valentine's Terror
Herbal Smoke Revolution: The Ultimate Guide to Nature's Cigarette Alternative

Winter's Wrath: The Complete Survival Blueprint for Extreme Freezes.

The Groundhog's Shadow: A Tale of Seasons
Burrowed Insights: Wisdom from the Groundhog
Sensual Strings: The Art of Erotic Bondage
Whispered Flames: Unlocking the Power of Fire Play
Forgotten Shadows: A Guide to Cryptids Lost to Time
Six Weeks of Secrets: Groundhog Day's Hidden Messages
Shadows and Cycles: Groundhog Day Reflections
The Art of Love Letters: Crafting the Perfect Message
Romantic Getaways at Home: Turning Your Space into Paradise
Purrfect Brews: A Cat Lover's Guide to Coffee and Companionship
The Groundhog's Wisdom: Timeless Lessons for Modern Life
The Shadow Oracle: Groundhog Day as a Predictor
Emerging from the Burrow: A Journey of Renewal
The Language of Love: Learning Your Partner's Love Style
Authorpreneur: The Ultimate Blueprint for Writing, Publishing, and Thriving as an Author
Weathering the Seasons: Groundhog Day Perspectives
Valentine's Day Magic: A Guide to Romantic Rituals
The Shadow Chronicles: Stories of Groundhog Day
Love and Laughter: Fun Games for Valentine's Day
AstroRealty: Unlocking the Stars for Property Success
The Groundhog's Path: A Guide to Seasonal Balance
Groundhog Day Diaries: Reflections in the Shadow
The Groundhog's Light: Illuminating the Path Ahead
Valentine's Traditions from Around the World
AI Wealth Revolution: Unlocking the Trillionaire Mindset
Love Rekindled: Reigniting Passion in Relationships
Single and Thriving: Self-Love on Valentine's Day
Emerald Legends: Mystical Tales of Ireland
Green Alchemy: Harnessing Nature's Magic
The Hearts of Horror: A Valentine's Day Nightmare

The Leprechaun's Guide to Wealth and Wisdom

Dancing with the Sidhe: Celebrating the Otherworld

Shamrocks and Shadows: Mysteries of the Green Isle

Emerald Energy: Harnessing Luck and Growth

The Gingerbread Golem's Valentine: A Sweetheart's Guide to Love and Enchantment

The Celtic Knot: Weaving Life and Destiny

Green Fire: Elemental Magic for St. Patrick's Day

Clover Chronicles: Finding Your Inner Luck

Ireland's Mystical Creatures: A Field Guide

Gingerbread Golem's Love Almanac

Prowl and Thrive: The Lion's Guide to Success

Love Alchemy: Transforming Your Life Through Heart Energy

WORLD DOMINATION: Woman's Rule 3:The New Life

The Midnight Rose: A Guide to Lunar Love Spells

The Forbidden Letters: Writing Your Own Love Prophecy

Luck and Lore: St. Patrick's Day for Modern Mystics

The Green Path: A Pagan Celebration of Renewal

The Dark Architect's Guide to Reprogramming Reality

Prankster's Paradise: A Guide to Harmless Hijinks

Manifest Your Reality: The Law of Attraction Simplified

The TARDIS Owner's Manual: Understanding the Doctor's Ship: *A complete guide to the TARDIS, its technology, secrets, and mysteries*

Starlit Romance: Astrology Secrets for Finding True Love

The Time Lord's Atlas: A Complete Guide to the Whoniverse: ***A breakdown of the locations, planets, and dimensions explored in Doctor Who***

Sweetheart Shadows: The Dark Side of Love and Attraction

February Fire: Reigniting Passion in Every Area of Life

The Self-Love Toolkit: 5 Ways to Embrace Who You Are

February Sparks: Ignite Your Dreams in 28 Days

March to Success: A 31-Day Action Blueprint
Ancient Paths: The 13 Sacred Principles of Dino Wicca
Echoes of Tomorrow: Navigating the AI Revolution
The Wellness Blueprint: Balancing Mind, Body, and Soul
Green Horizons: Sustainable Living for a Better Tomorrow
The AI Wealth Code: How to Make Millions with Automation
AI-Powered Creativity: Writing, Art, and Music for Profit
Extinction Rites: Rebirthing Your Soul Through Prehistoric Magick
Sacred Serpents tarot
Celestial Enchantment blank journal
Star Strains
Culinary Journeys: Exploring Global Flavors at Home
The Hollowvale Curse
The Hollowvale Harvest
The Egg of Transformation: Awakening Your Inner Power
Blooming Into Power: A Wiccan Guide to Spring Awakening
The Nightmare Nexus: The Third Doctor's Perilous Haunting
Digital Detox: Reclaiming Your Life in a Connected World
Ostara's Path: Walking the Spiral of Renewal
The Sacred Hare
Financial Freedom: Building Wealth in the Modern Age
Spring's Cauldron: Stirring the Waters of Change
The Hollowvale Pact
Quantum Consciousness: The Science of Reality Shifting
The Hollowvale Hunger
The Sacred Waters Within: A Witch's Guide to Hydrocephalus Magick
The Raven's Nest: Building a Life of Unshakable Stability
AI and the Human Mind: The Future of Intelligence
The Hollowvale Reckoning
Timeless Love: Building and Maintaining Lasting Relationships

The Raven's Roar: Unlocking Unstoppable Confidence
Raven Sight: Awakening Intuition and Inner Wisdom
The Butterfly Effect: Small Changes, Big Transformations
Taming the Boogeyman: How to Conquer Your Inner Fears
The Magick of Green: Awakening Earth's Energy in You
The Entrepreneurial Mindset: Secrets to Business Success
The Hollowvale End
The Shadow Luck Ritual: Reclaiming Power from Your Dark Side
Spring Magick for Beginners: A Simple Guide to Seasonal Energy Work
Doctor Who: The Hollowvale Conundrum
The March of Miracles: Unlocking Synchronicities in Spring
Unveiling the Cosmos: A Guide to Stargazing and Space Exploration
The Ultimate Guide to Surviving an Economic Collapse
The AI Gold Rush: How to Profit from the AI Revolution
Bastet's Shadow: The Hidden Power of Feline Magick
The Bastet Codex: Unlocking the Goddess's Magickal Secrets
Purring Spells: Harnessing Bastet's Healing Frequencies
Bastet's Nine Lives: Rebirth, Transformation, and Immortality Spells
Primal Currents: Hydrocephalus Magick in the Path of Dino Wicca
The Digital Gold Rush: Mastering E-Commerce and Online Sales
Future Shock: Adapting to the Next Decade of Change
The Quantum Mindset: Think Like a Billionaire
Sacred Motherhood: Awakening the Divine Feminine Within
The Mother's Spellbook: Enchantments for Love, Protection, and Prosperity
The Witch's Guide to Parenting: Raising Empowered and Intuitive Children

The Magick of Motherhood: Reclaiming Your Power Through Rituals
The Pagan Path to Self-Love: A Goddess's Guide to Worth and Confidence
Wild Woman Magick: Unleashing Your Primal Power
The Money Magnet Blueprint: Unlocking Unlimited Wealth
Biohacking 101: Unlock Your Body's Full Potential
The Wild Father: A Pagan Guide to Strength and Wisdom
The Sacred Masculine: Unlocking Your Inner Power
The Druid's Compass
The Warrior's Mindset
The Father's Fire
Odin's Path
Ancestral Bonds
The House That Whispers
The Magician's Code
The Wild Hunt
The Green Man's Path
The Altar of Success
The Shadow and the Sword
The High Priestess's Guide to Energy Healing
The Lunar Mother
The Sacred Self-Care Grimoire
The Womb Wisdom Codex
The Wheel of the Mother
The Witch's Guide to Manifestation
The Q2 Reset
The Ultimate Guide to AI-Powered Passive Income
Escape the 9-5
AI Feline Fortunes
The Tear-Stained Grimoire
Razorblade Runes
Cemetery Sirens

The Midnight Wristwatch
The Town That Forgets
AI Horror & Creepypasta
The Hollow Frequency
The Breach Echo
The Quiet Between Worlds
The Sigil of Tharan-Khul
Summon the Vault of Y'ha'ten
The Becoming Codex
The Profit of Az'ra-nar
The Drowned Logos
Echoes of the Eldritch Will
The Deep Ledger
Necronomicon of Networth
Covenant of the Wealthwyrm
The Whisperer's Manifesto
The Rites of Azh-K'luth
The Ark of the Crawling Coin
The Tithe of Shadows
Inkheart Abyss
The Timewinds of Y'ha-nthlei
The Spiral Labyrinth of Azag-Nirrh
The Gallifreyan Heresy of the Black Pharaoh
The Psalms of Nyog-Sotha
Black Rain Alchemy
The Infinite Maw
The Entropic Blueprint
The Oracle of Sh'guul
The Book of Breach
The Drowned Saint's Testament
Dreamcraft of the Sleeper God
The Silence Market
Cthonomics: The Dark Wealth Algorithm

Invocation of the Ten-Eyed King
Wealthbound to the Wyrm Below
Become the Unnameable
Codex of the Sovereign Flame
Rituals of Relentless Becoming
The Shadow Ascends
The Eyes Beneath You
The Will That Wakes Worlds
Silence Is a Weapon
The Mirror That Screams
The Whisper Between Moments
The Mind That Devours Fear
The Myth of the Finished Self
The Architect of Your Madness
The Voice You've Buried
The Discipline of Madness
Stormborn: Awakening Your Inner Tempest
The Mind That Ate Time
Unbind Your Becoming
The Pact You Owe Yourself
The Devourer's Diet
The Acid That Carves the Path
The Tower You Must Burn
The Breath Between Worlds
Speak Like the Deep
The Labyrinth Within
The Spine of the Sea God
Rejection Is a Portal
The Crown You Refused
The Scar Is the Spell
The Lightless Flame
The Habit of Becoming Horrific
ChickenJockey Chaos

The Gatekeeper Within
You Are Not Your Name
The Compass of the Mad
The Archive of Unsent Letters
What the Mirror Can't Show You
The Knife You Needed
Worship Nothing, Become Everything
The Other Voice
The Body the World Forgot
The Vein of the Void
The Black Bone Codex
The Puzzle of the Hidden Self (Millennium Puzzle)
The Eye That Sees the Lie *(Millennium Eye)*
The Ring of Return (Millennium Ring)
The Rod of Relentless Will ***(Millennium Rod)***
The Tally of the Soul (Millennium Tauk/Necklace)
The Key to the Locked Timeline (Millennium Key)
The Scale of Sacred Decisions (Millennium Scales)
Inferno Bites: The UnOfficial Minecraft Lava Cookbook
Rot in the Attic
Prana: The Hidden Force of Your Infinite Self
The Shadow Realm Within: Transforming Darkness Into Destiny
The Borderland Collapse
Claws of Protection: Bastet's Defensive Magick
Mr. Ring-a-Ding's Madness
Yugioh Astrology: Celestial Deckcraft and Duel Destiny (2026–2027 Edition)
The Seal You Signed: Unlocking the Power You Once Feared
The Puzzle of Infinite Minds: Unlocking the Mentalism Hidden Within
The Eye That Mirrors the All: Secrets of Inner Reflection
Doctor Who: The Toymaker's Broadcast

Rootwake: The Carbon Covenant
Skitter Logic: Unlearning the Fear That Built You
Doctor Who: The World That Froths
Rootwake: The Fizz That Rewrites Flesh
Rootwake: Frothfather of the World
The Holly Pact: Blood Beneath the Mistletoe
The 2nd Mass Principle: Building Unbreakable Tribes
Web of Wits: A Survival Guide to Encounters with Anasi the Spider (Aunt Nancy)
The Hexbreaking Handbook: Effective Spells to Remove Curses
Pop Alchemy: Transform Your Life One Sip at a Time
The Mason Code: Leading in Unleadable Times
Petosiris and the Fifth Chamber of Thoth
The Ether Seed Within
The Parent of Tomorrow
Petosiris's Pyramid of Perpetual Wealth
Unlearn the World
Grimoire of the Hollow Tongue
Zodiac Weeds: Finding Your Strain Through the Stars
Aquarius Rises in the Bank
The Sugar God's Smile
The Skinclock Reversal: Biohacking the Face of Time
Debtburn: How to Obliterate What You Owe Forever
The Ice Cream Oracle: What Your Cone Says About Your Future
Silence Is Sovereignty: The Power of Being Unreadable
The Wind That Whispers Through Stone
Path of the Four Directions
Doctor Who: The Maestro's Symphony of Endings
Oxygen Grail: Breathing to Undo the Clock
Zodiacal Collapse: When Stars Devour Time
Teachings from the Red Sand Silence

Doctor Who: Omega – The Broken Equation
Memory Wipe Your Past: Start Over Like a MiB
Mitochondria Prime: Ignite the Core of Youth
A Nest of Roaches
Grub from the Galaxy: MiB Recipes You'll Never Forget
Whiskers of Power: Bastet's Guide to Inner Sovereignty
The Gift Must Cost Them: Negotiation Through Unequal Exchange
The Worm Guys' Wealth Code: Hustle Like an Alien
Bug Out: The Edgar Method for Ruthless Goal Setting
Weaving Life with Spiderwoman's Pattern
Doctor Who: The Rani's Renaissance
How to Get a Job (If You're a Puppygirl)
Speak Through Others: The Art of Proxy Power
T-Rex Your Trauma: Reclaim the Power of Your Primal Self
The Black Briefcase: How MiB Stay Wealthy in Silence
The Thirst Beyond Reason: Understanding Diabetes Insipidus From the Inside Out
Backwoods Witchcraft for Billionaires: The Pagan Path from Dirt Roads to Gold Roads
The Moonshine Grimoire: Fermented Spells for Abundance
The Nameless Geometry
The Wraith's Mixtape: Spellcasting with Songs of Sorrow
The Gallifreyan Gentleman: Silent Wealth, Sonic Confidence, and the Doctor's Code of Living
Sugar Water Confidence
Dino Totems: Spirit Guides from Earth's First Gods
Pumpkin Sigils & Ritual Smoke
The Hózhó Compass
The Distortus Discipline – Order from Inner Mutation
Witchcraft for the Cold-Blooded Soul
Moonlight Over the Blessingway
Water, Interrupted: When the Body Forgets How to Hold On

Deformed but Divine: Embracing Your Asymmetry

Hexes in the Henhouse: The Farm Witch's Guide to Power

The Reversed Flame: A Grimoire of Inverted Power

Salt, Cells, and Sanity: Reclaiming Balance with Diabetes Insipidus

King of the Broken: Crowning the Flawed Self

Moonlight Scars: Emo Moon Magick and the Art of Lunar Sorrow

Noose Spells: Magick of the Hanging Rope

The Goth Cathedral: Rituals of the Broken and Beautiful

The Cretaceous Codex: Dino Spirits and Fossil Magick

The Turkey Bones Ritual

Nine Lives of Manifestation: Unlocking Bastet's Reality Codes

Chaos Muscles: Building Strength from Twisted Pain

Emo Blood Magick: The Veins of Power

The 3AM Flood: Nighttime Urination, Sleep Loss, and the DI Spiral

The Silence Between the Stars

The Lemon Method: Sour Your Way to Success

Starlit Sovereign

The Rite of Twelve Gates: Walking the Gates of the Duat.

Cornbread and Conjure: Recipes for Riches and Rootwork

The Black Rose Rituals: Emo Love Spells and Obsession Magick

The Eternal Goodbye: Death Magick and Rebirth Rituals

Sinkrot: The Drain That Remembers

The Hybrid Mindset: Thinking Beyond Evolution

Bone Dry: Navigating Dehydration Before It Breaks You

Wreathcraft: Winter Sigils and Yuletide Spells

The Rite of Twelve Mouths

S'mores of the Damned: Haunted Recipes for Halloween Night

Rethink the Drink: A Beverage Survival Guide for DI Warriors

The Shadow Chord: Guitar Magick and Sonic

Malformed Yet Majestic: Leading When You Feel Wrong Inside

The Cursed Diary: Ink-Stained Spells of the Emo Soul

Anxiety Off Switch: Emergency Reset for a Fried Nervous System

The Energy Heist: How to Take Back Your Life from Drainers

Beyond the Bathroom: Rebuilding Your Social Life With DI

Coyote's Gift for Decision Makers

Ghoul-Goo: Spooky S'mores You'll Die For

Echoes in the Mirror: Scrying and Self-Destruction Magick

Thread and Thorn: Stitching Spells from Rural Cloth

The Mogwai Mind: Building Untouchable Wealth from Small Ideas

Be Your Own Guide: Trust Your Inner Compass

Hormones in Chaos: The Endocrine Puzzle of Diabetes Insipidus

ChronoCleanse: Detox Your Biological Timeline

The Limb You Hide Is the One That Saves You

Leaves, Bones, and Whisper Spells

The Dinosaur Mindset: Prehistoric Tactics for Modern Wealth

Clawing Back Control: A Bastet Method for Boundaries and Empowerment

Samhain Codes of the Forgotten

Orange Alchemy: The Autumnal Spellbook

Monster Within, Master Without

The Sigil That Sleeps

Hearthcraft: Yule Hearth Sigils and Winter Warmth Spells

Temple of the Purring Moon: Rituals from Bastet's Lineage

When the Earth Remembers Your Footsteps

Food for Mood: Eat to Heal Depression, Not Just Survive It
Witch of the Kudzu Vine: Southern Pagan Wealth Secrets
The Invisible Diagnosis: Advocating for Yourself With DI
The Coffin's Lullaby: Sleep Magick and Nightmares as Portals
Ashes of the Will: Rituals for Erasing the Self
The Fracture Rite: Shattering the Magickal Core
Funeral Candles: The Art of Emo Flame Magick
The Black Grimoire: A Blank Ritual for Writing in Absence
Phantom Thirst: A Halloween Survival Guide for Diabetes Insipidus
The Hollow Crown: Emo Royalty and Magick of the Outcast King
Sandpainting for the Soul
Falling Into Balance: Using the Extra Hour to Recalibrate Life
100 Southern Superstitions That Still Work
The DI Child: A Parent's Guide to Raising Hydrated, Happy Kids
The Jungle of Shame: Escaping the Hidden Lab of Doubt
The Witch's Toast: S'mores Spells and Creepy Confections
The Hoodoo Pantry: Spells from the Mason Jar
The Immortal Fortune: Secret Wealth Lessons from Captain Jack Harkness
The Specter's Embrace: Magick for Channeling Ghostly Lovers
Grateful Waters: A Thanksgiving Survival Guide for Diabetes Insipidus
The Seizure Gospel
Harvestbind: Autumn Sigils and Samhain Spells
Doctor Who: The Algorithmic Awakening
Silent Nights, Steady Waters: A Christmas Survival Guide for Diabetes Insipidus
The Extra Hour Effect: How One Hour Can Transform Everything

Blade Between the Breaths
Running with the Mountain Shadows
Echoes of the Failed Experiment – Becoming a Living Legacy
Swamp Witches & River Ghosts: Real Southern Hauntings
Cornbread Prophecies: Magical Recipes from a Southern Table
Doctor Who: The Signal in the Star
Bloomcraft: Spring Sigils and Equinox Enchantments
Vanisher: How to Disappear from the Internet Without Losing Your Life
The Ultimate Christmas Cookie Cookbook
The Unbreakable Parent: How to Mentally Survive Raising Kids in a Broken World
Time Debt: How to Reclaim the Hours You Didn't Know You Lost
One Month, One Million: Unconventional Cash Creation Tactics
Doctor Who: The Cyber Conversion Protocol
Black Friday Frenzy: The Art of Finding Hidden Online Deals
The Grimoire Buried Under the Apple Tree

Get Some Tarot cards: https://www.makeplayingcards.com/sell/apophis-occult-shop

Get some shirts: https://www.bonfire.com/store/apophis-shirt-emporium/

<u>Instagrams:</u>
@apophis_enterprises,
@apophisbookemporium,
@apophisscardshop
Twitter: @apophisenterpr1
Tiktok:@apophisenterprise
Youtube: @sg1fan23477
Hive: @sg1fan23477
CheeLee: @SG1fan23477

Podcast: Apophis Chat Zone: https://open.spotify.com/show/5zXbrCLEV2xzCp8ybrfHsk?si=fb4d4fdbdce44dec

Newsletter: https://apophiss-newsletter-27c897.beehiiv.com/

If you want to support me or see posts of other projects that I have come over to: **buymeacoffee.com/mpetchinskg**

I post there daily several times a day

Get your Dinowicca or Christmas themed digital products, especially Santa Raptor songs and other musics. Here: **https://sg1fan23477.gumroad.com**

Apophis Yuletide Digital has not only digital Christmas items, but it will have all things with Dinowicca as well as other Digital products.

www.ingramcontent.com/pod-product-compliance
Lightning Source LLC
LaVergne TN
LVHW022010200926
848481LV00007B/2323
* 9 7 9 8 3 3 0 4 2 3 0 1 9 *